AF560338

CARTWHEEL BOOKS
An Imprint of Scholastic Inc.

For Marcus—stay inspired!
—T.A.

ISBN 978-93-5471-231-9

Printed in India

First printing, September 2013

This reprint edition: September 2024

A boy had a pet fly
named Fly Guy.
Fly Guy could say
the boy's name—

One night Buzz said,
"I made a book.
We are the superheroes."

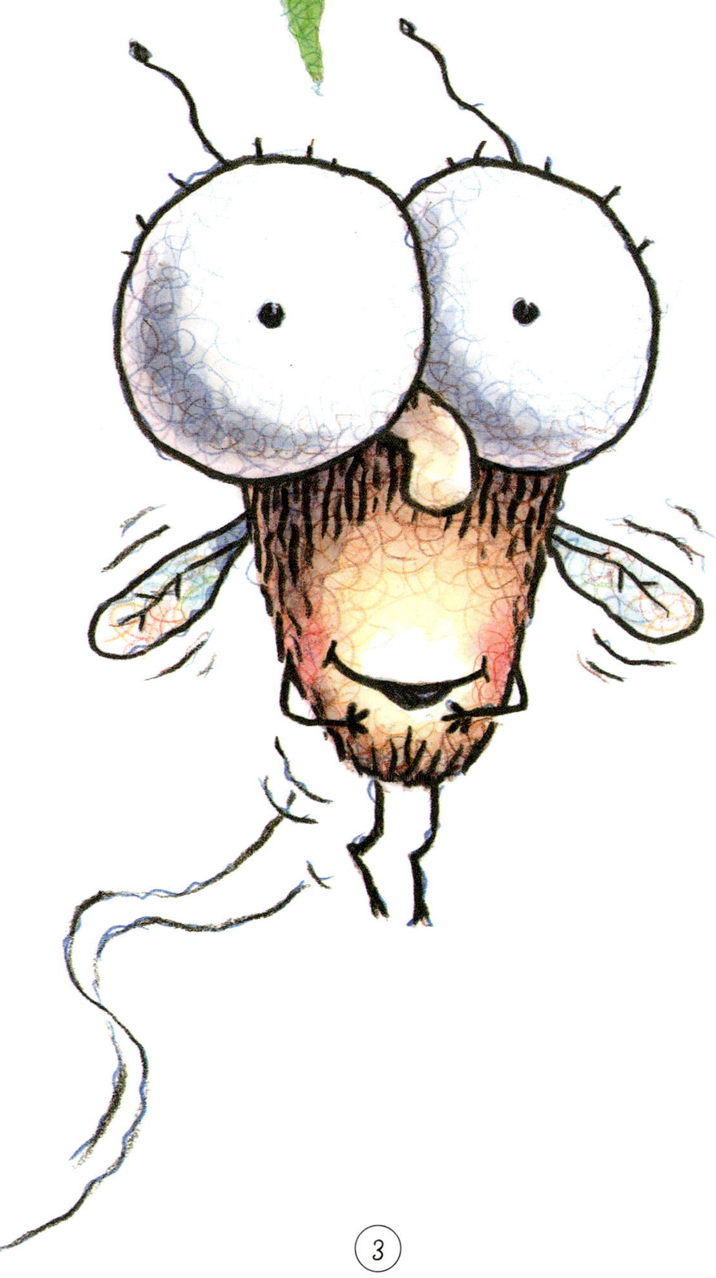
HEROZZZZ?

"Yes," said Buzz.

"I'll read it to you."

THE AMAZING ADVENTURES OF BUZZ BOY AND FLY GUY
FG
BB
BY ME (BUZZ)

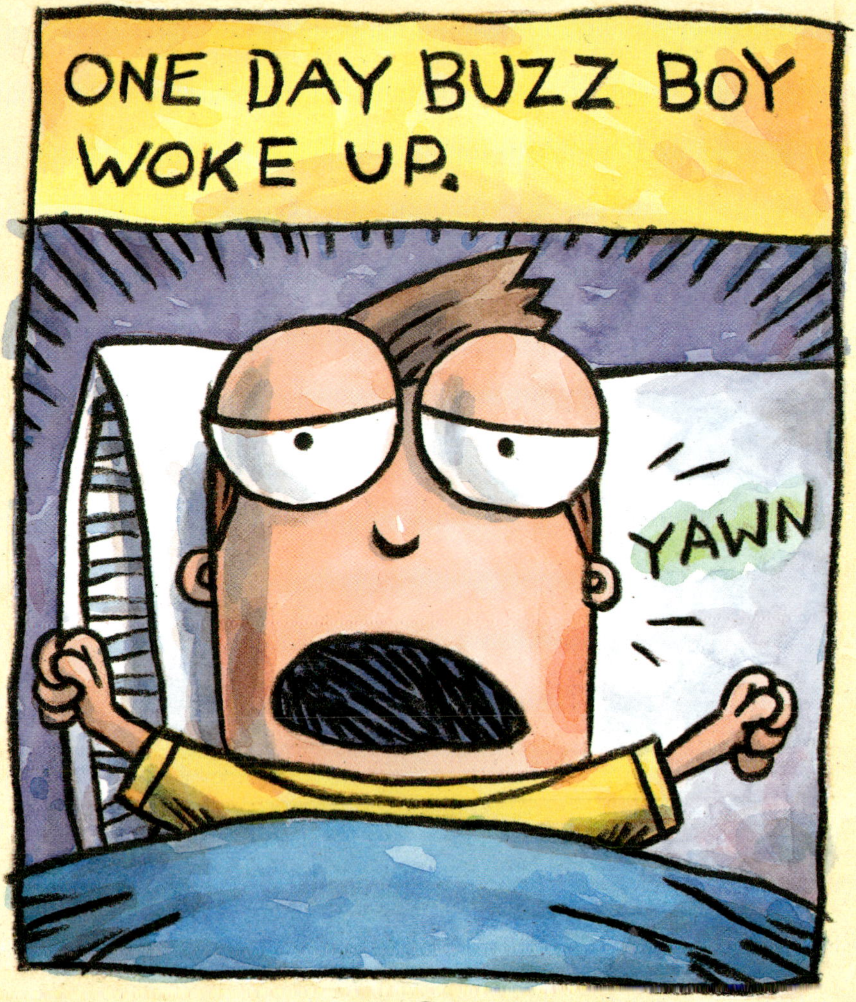

ONE DAY BUZZ BOY WOKE UP.

YAWN

HE WAS THE SAME SIZE AS FLY GUY!

I HAVE BAD NEWS!
FLY GUY CAN TALK!

WHAT?

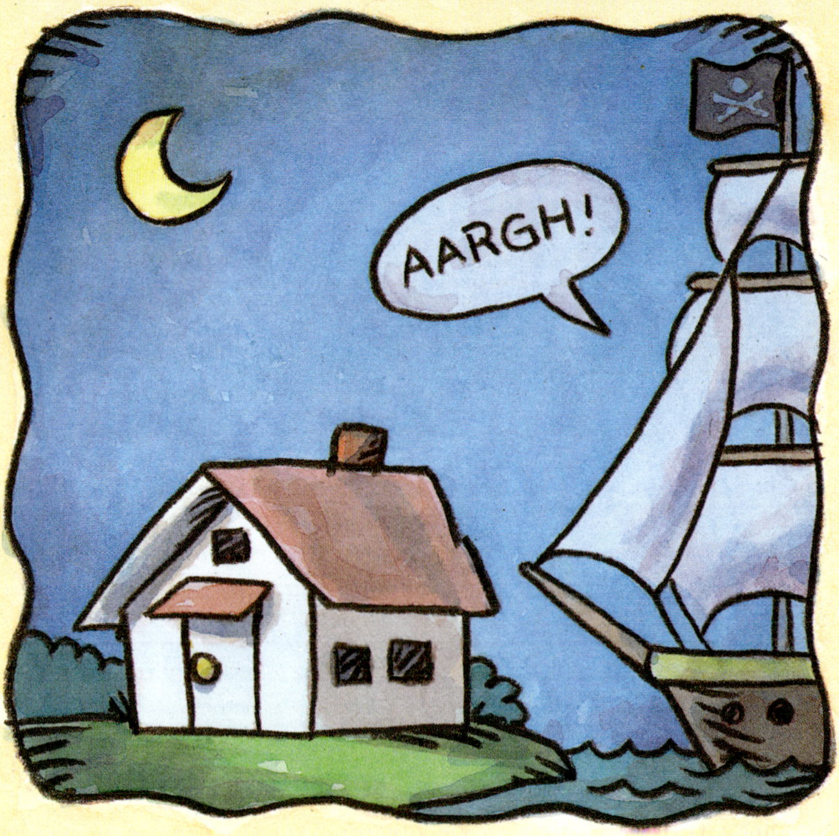

AARGH!

THEY TOOK OUR HOUSE TO A DRAGON CAVE...
AARGH!

PIRATE GUARDS
MORE PIRATES
ON AN ISLAND FAR AWAY.

BUZZ BOY LOOKED OUT THE WINDOW.

HE SAW A SLEEPING DRAGON.

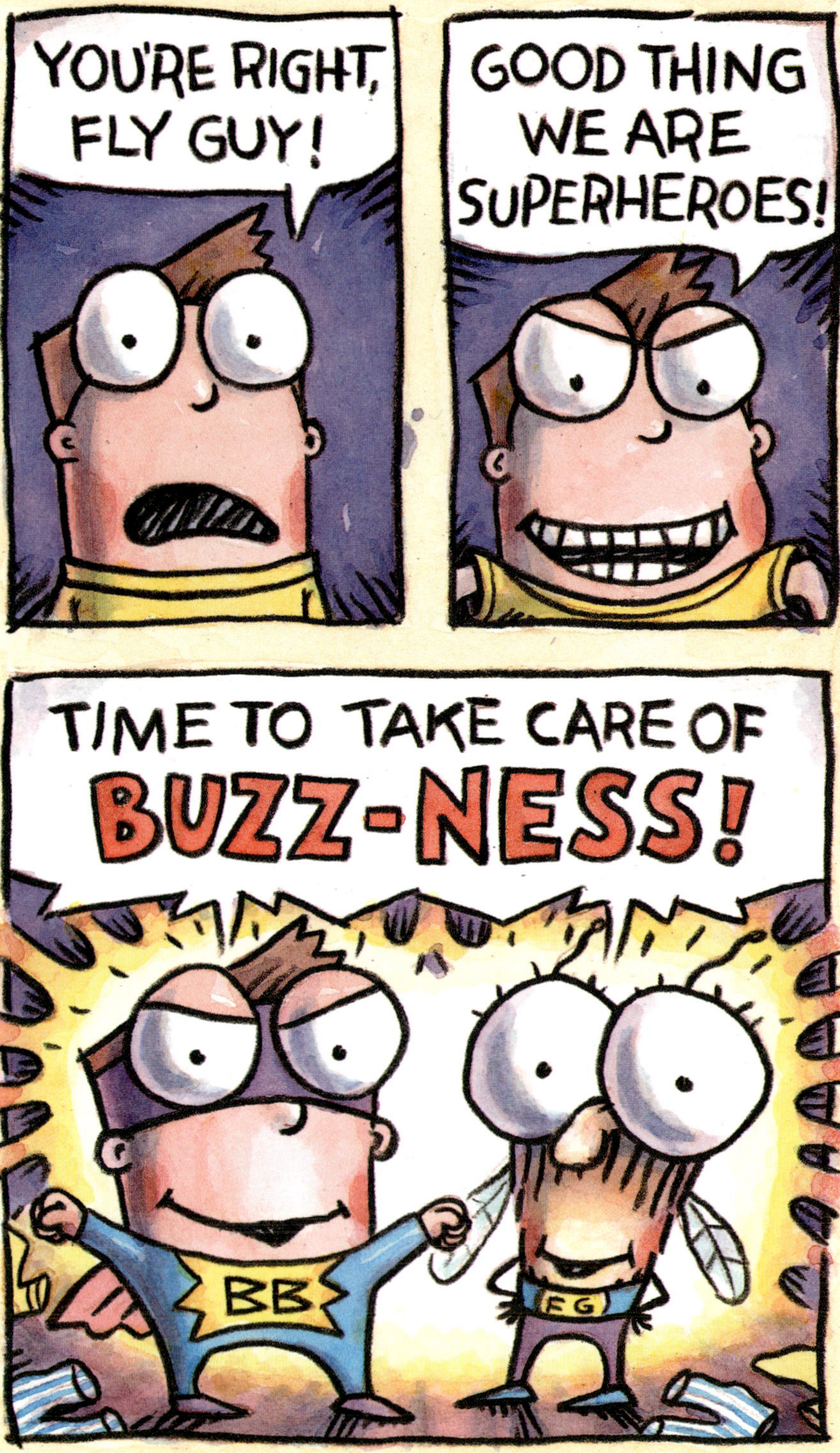

TIME TO TAKE CARE OF BUZZ-NESS!

BB

FG

CHAPTER
TWO

THE DRAGON WAS STILL ASLEEP.
BB

WITH HIS SUPERSTRENGTH
BUZZ BOY TURNED THE
DRAGON AROUND.
BB

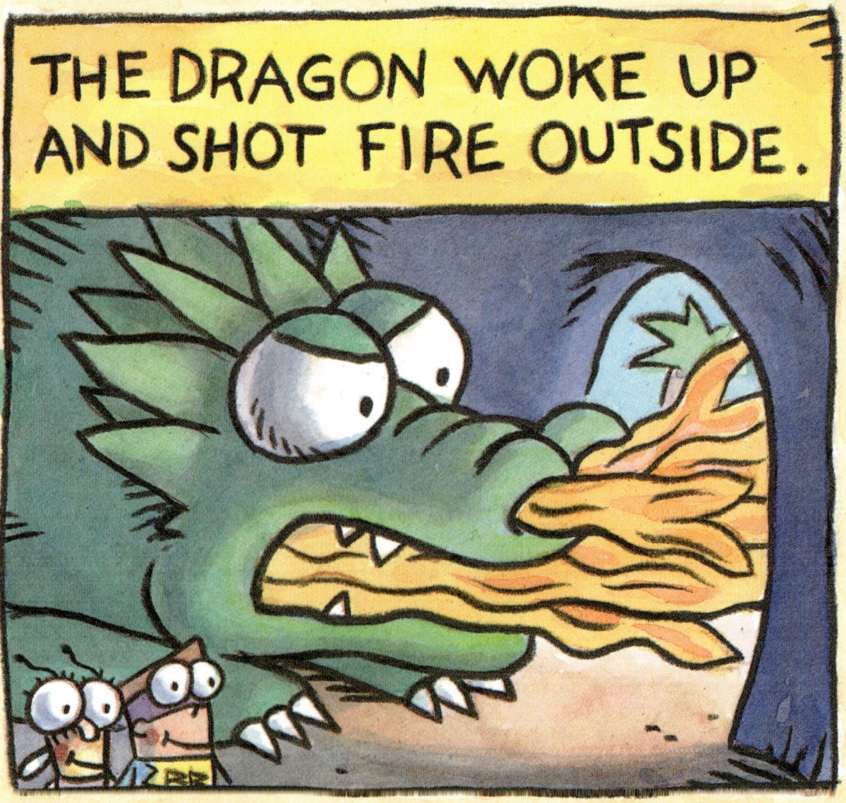

THE DRAGON WOKE UP AND SHOT FIRE OUTSIDE.

THE PIRATE GUARDS RAN AWAY.

OOPS! MORE PIRATES!

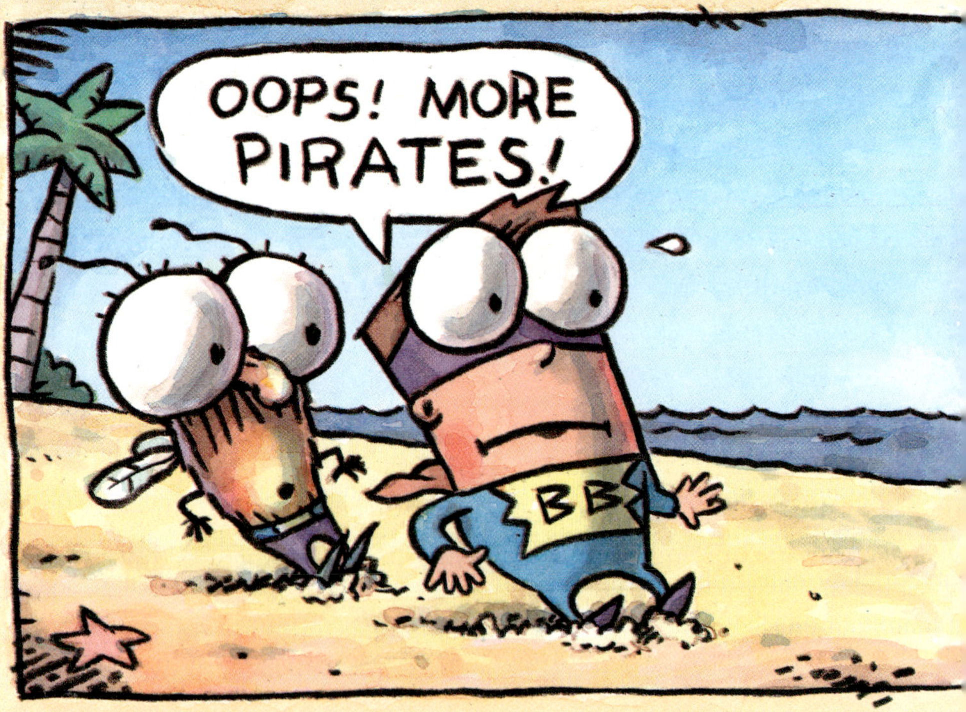

AARGH!

BUZZ BOY AND FLY GUY WERE PUT IN JAIL ON THE PIRATE SHIP.

SUPER SKELETON KEY!

FLY GUY UNLOCKED THE DOOR.
YIKES! WE ARE AT THE TOP OF THE PIRATE SHIP!

GOOD THING WE CAN **BOTH** FLY!!!

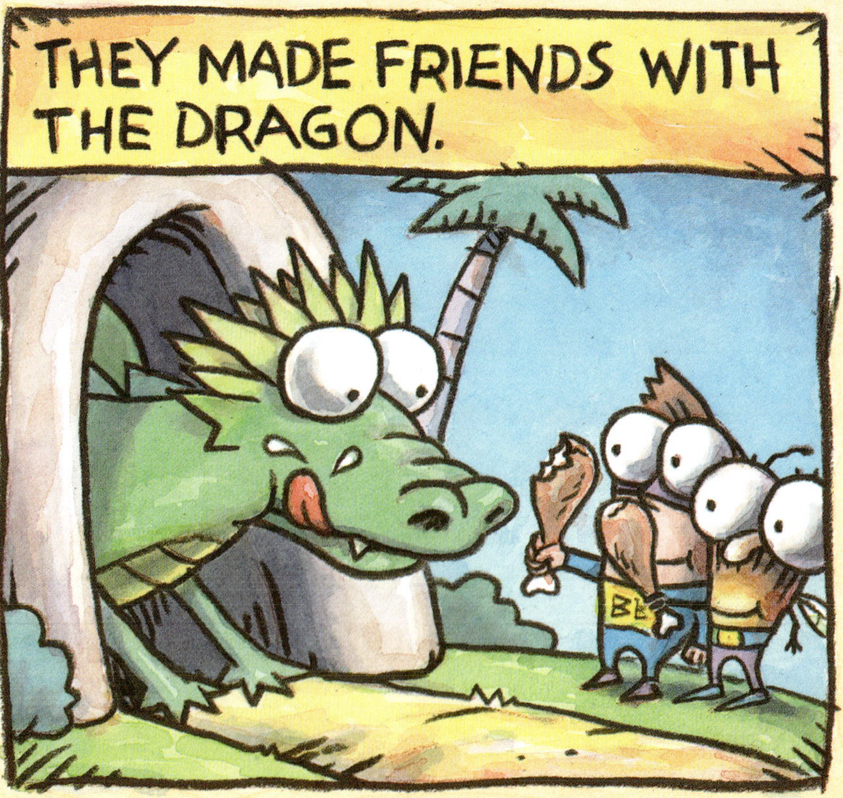

THEY MADE FRIENDS WITH THE DRAGON.

THE DRAGON TOOK THEIR HOUSE BACK HOME.

BUZZ BOY AND FLY GUY LET THE DRAGON JOIN THEIR TEAM.
DRAGON DUDE!
DD
BB
FG

"The end," said Buzz.

Fly Guy said,

"Superheroes," said Buzz.
"Want to read it again?"